JUST LiKE
마치

Just Like

by Lee Sumyeong

Translated by Colin Leemarshall

Black Ocean
Boston · Chicago

Black Ocean
P.O. Box 52030
Boston, MA 02205
blackocean.org

Cover Art and Design by Abby Haddican | abbyhaddican.com
Book Design by Taylor D. Waring | taylordwaring.com

ISBN: 9781939568755
Library of Congress Control Number: 2024930338

This book is published with the support of the Literature Translation Institute of Korea (LTI Korea).

Printed in Canada

FIRST EDITION

CONTENTS

3.

TRANSLATOR'S INTRODUCTION: JUST LIKE AS IF

In the spring of 2019, I chanced upon Lee Sumyeong's book "마치" [*machi*] in a small campus bookstore. What initially drew my attention was the book's clipped adverbial title, which stood out both for its brevity and for its defiant lack of "poetic" ballast. Picking up the book and opening it to the first poem, I proceeded to read something like the following:

THINGS LIKE CEMENT VEGETABLE PAPER

A man runs a field and the field of the man running the field caves in. A man lacking a caved-in field to the man runs. Things like cement vegetable paper sweltering he haphazardly plucks cabbage. Picks up the cabbage and walks the field a man bored through.

The mice escaping the field to escape the field is uncomfortable.

A man runs a field and because the field has no lid the era of the field closes the man. Closes the field. The man running the field drags over the field. The field is an expanding use. Into the man the man is ousted. Brings up things like cement vegetable paper.

Even though I was already in my mid-30s at the time, my encounter with Lee's poem strikes me on reflection as having been somehow formative. The strangeness of the poem—its uncanny grammar; its entanglements of man and field; its subtle yet vast thematic implicature; its permutational richness—hit me almost immediately. By that point, I had been living in Korea for just under a decade, and I had already been intermittently translating Korean poetry (albeit in a quite dilettantish manner and without any plans for publication) for several years. But reading Lee's poem, I felt something that I had not felt previously—a *compulsion* to translate, perhaps even a *need* to translate.

Looking back, I recognize the intensity of this response as the first stirring of a kind of psychic imprimatur—a reflexive license to translate something *seriously* for the first time in my life. In my previous dabblings with translation, I had convinced myself that the practice was not something that, for me, could ever amount to more than a private diversion. While doubts about my Korean ability were surely a factor in my trepidation, I now realize that the mental blockage stemmed not purely from concerns about competency or aptness; it was also the result of a certain literary pessimism—a pessimism of which Lee's book, more so than any other, has since succeeded in disabusing me. This change was triggered in part by the cognitive polarities that Lee's poetry elicits. On the one hand, there is an undeniable immediacy to the poems: not only are they comparatively pared down in terms of diction, but they are also largely free of any discursive or allusive freight. But from clarity comes confusion—crystalline sentences give way to complex run-on syntagms; grammatical moods shift without warning; conjunctive clauses prove tenuous or illogical; poems end abruptly or with apparent non-sequiturs. For whatever reason, this dichotomy between order and confusion made me feel that genuine ingress into the world of translation had suddenly become more possible.

I. From Homeophrase to Allopoem

Before the first poem proper in "마치," there is a highly suggestive sliver of prefatory matter:

3월, 행진, 망치,

그리고
Als Ob

This preface seems designed both to repel a facile translation and to highlight *translation itself* as being somehow key to the poetics of the book. In a mere handful of words, there are tinctures of multiple scripts or languages: Arabic, Korean, Chinese, English, German, and Latin. The "literal" semantic translation of the words is "March, march, hammer / and [also] / as if." Transliterated, the Korean words read: "sawol, haengjin, mangchi / geurigo." If examined purely from the point of view of their semantic and phonological Korean properties, the words in the first string bear seemingly no relation to each other. However, in the process of translating the first two words into English, one can quickly discern what some theorists would call the *tertium comparationis* (hereafter "tertium"), the "factor which links or is the common ground between two elements in comparison" (*OED*). The tertium in this instance is the English word "March/march" qua its analysis into the phonetic unit "maːtʃ." Appropriately, the link is weak, identifiable only via a kind of recognized *difference* whereby the monosyllabic "maːtʃ" bends according to the rules of Korean phonology, becoming the bisyllabic "machi" [마치] of the book's title. Thus, the language that is translated *out of* is almost instantaneously translated *back into*. All of this is carried out furtively: "March" and "march" exist merely as *implied* translations, while "마치" is observable only via its deformation into the word "망치" (hammer), whose jamo "ㅇ" functions both as the welt of the violence and the instrument of it, in addition to which it further reinforces the spoliation by turning the syllable into a homophone of the Sinitic "亡" (destroy, collapse, etc.). There is a similar play in the remaining lines: "Als Ob" bears a graphical similarity to "also" (a latent translation of "그리고"), such that we might say that it is *as if* one locution were potentially *just like* the other—or, given the refractory capitals, the typographical space, and the appended "b," as if it were *almost* just like the other. Within this brief textual field, then, there is a kind of semantico-phonological shell game going on, by which the kernel of likeness engendered by the word relationships keeps shifting into mere similarity. On the one hand, the strategic arrangement of Lee's words suggests that a hyper-translation of them might read "마치, 마치, 마치, / 마치 / 마치" (or "as if, as if, as if, / as if / as if", etc.). But the lines are also set up to resolutely thwart such a translation, to deny the *machi* or the *als ob* or the *as if* within their midst.

This preface heralds one of the major concerns of Lee's book—how within the concept of likeness there is an inherent vacillation between identity and difference. While translating the collection, I thought constantly about distinctions between the *homo-* (the same) and the *homeo-* (the similar). It is perhaps worth noting that these two combining forms bear a strong resemblance to each other, and they can in certain guises appear almost indistinguishable.[1] Likewise, words and phrases in *Just Like* constantly hover between these contiguous states of identity and similarity. A few excerpts will hopefully prove illustrative:

between new gradation and gradation
pointing at similar gradation ("raise arm")

just like
dead leaves will surely cover the ground
dead leaves will surely cover the ground completely [. . .]
just like
as if overflowing ("just like")

into a complex into a complex
crying children enter and because the complex spills out

there are so many complexes so
they are living in the same complex ("residents")

Note first the lines "just like / as if overflowing." On the one hand, the simile is placed at a further remove from the referent via the conjunctive doubling, while on the other hand it seems to overflow into the referent via the suggestiveness of the line break. An examination of the other excerpts can help us clarify this condition still further. Collectively, this suite of quotations would seem to suggest that Lee is strongly drawn to the rhetorical figure of epizeuxis—the proximate repetition of words or phrases. It should be noted that Korean admits of repetition more readily than English does—whereas the latter tends to eschew nominal repetition and opt instead for endophoric pronouns or the like, the former is more forgiving of lexical reduplication. Korean is also far more homeostatic in terms of its sound culminations—sentence endings are conventionally fixed or limited, tending in the written language to culminate with a "-다" (da) particle. In this way, Korean comes pre-installed with something akin to what, since Aristotle's *Rhetoric*, has been known as homoioteleuton (or homeoteleuton), repetition of the same or similar word endings. But if Lee is already operating within a linguistic system that is comparatively built for repetition, her repetitions nonetheless move strikingly beyond those that are standard in the language. Instead of mere nominal reduplication or inbuilt line-ending repetition, there is something like a confluence of the two, a significant or wholesale repetition of word or phrase—something that we might call *homeophrasis*. A homeophrastic line works differently to an epizeuctic one; whereas epizeuxis is rhetorically concerned with emphasis or reiteration, homeophrasis is predicated on ontological mutability or uncertainty. Thus, "gradation" can be *similar to* or *identical with* "gradation"; to "cover the ground" and to "cover the ground completely" can be "just like" each other, even if neither is propositionally sufficient; and "so many [different] complexes" can simultaneously be "the same complex." For Lee, the homeophrase is one of the fundamental units of a poetics in which image, referent, and category constantly flicker between uniqueness and equivalence, between form and nebulosity, between immanence and its evacuation.

> the night drives everything into the night.
> The night returns to the night and
> along with the night the night is completely full. ("night's formation
> fliers")

This poetics of similarity expands beyond the homeophrase up to the level of the poem itself. Like elusive dreams, Lee's poems are often no more than semi-apprehensible. When we fall asleep or wake up, the opposed logics of dream and wakefulness coalesce into a hypnagogic pool in which things become "without reason":

> Woke slowly. Woke crying. Tears fell without reason from within sleep. The shoulders are scattered. Who was crying who was briefly hidden there are times even when I'm a girl times even when morning becomes perforated. When morning appears give me morning. Well-known costumes were invariably established I keep wanting to be your costume. Since the future initially passed we continued to use the future. Throwing the beach ball the girls are reiterated and who was briefly hidden who was crying I want to be your empty beach ball. Today misplaced sleep. I fit wherever. ("someone briefly")

As elsewhere in Lee's poetry, the syntactic unfolding is highly mutable, with short, clear sentences nestling against mercurial syntagms that forgo punctuation. While much modern poetry eschews the full stop altogether, Lee incorporates it into almost all of her poems—never as an atavistic feature, but rather as a highly estranging device whose demarcating energies are as much fluid, oblique, and arbitrary as they are propositionally terminal. Such syntactic vacillation provides a good foil for the above poem, wherein the attempt to relay an oneiric scene is full of porosity, dispersal, and confusion. The awakened crier cannot uncomplicatedly be the agent of the crying, as the tears fall "from within sleep." But neither is it the case that there is a monolithic dream-crier. Just as the lines juxtapose multiple modal conditions (interrogative, indicative, optative) and undulate between various temporal horizons, so too does the "I" shift (or potentially shift) to various loci ("girl," "costume," "empty beach ball," "today," etc.). In short, the rendering into language bilaterally compromises the waking and the dream states, obscuring the essence of what is being described—there is similarity, perhaps, but too much uncertainty for there to be identity or identification.

This uncertainty, which runs throughout *Just Like*, has the effect of suggesting that Lee's poems are not quite resolved. Both within and outside of the poems there are, I believe, *other poems*, variants of the given, secret iterations occulted in the undertows of disintegrative logic, isomorphic grammar, surreptitious homophony, and various other phenomena. Such *allopoems*, as I will call them, should not be understood as being akin to Platonic forms, ideals towards which the given poems stand merely as defective simulacra (such an idea would imply a conceptual purity that I do not think obtains in Lee's poetry). Nor are they rejectamenta akin to the negations of apophatic theology—dross removable from the ore so that we might get closer to the refulgent metal of the given poem. Instead, allopoems are potentially *constitutive* of the given poem, even if they are not perceivable. A somewhat crude analogy might be the biological phenotype—the observable set of traits exhibited by an organism. Just as beneath the phenotype there can be hidden traits in the genotype, so too do Lee's poems harbor unexpressed possibilities. As the problematizing deictic markers in the poem "carries me" hint, we should be wary about suffusing a given space with too tangible an immanence: "Even if I enter here here does not come to me [. . .] here being at there there being at over there." In other words, allopoetic features are part of a given poem even if they are elsewhere. Because of this condition, it is possible to describe the aggregate of allopoems within a given poem as the tertium by which the given poem becomes comparable to itself.

Logically speaking, the above claim is of course absurd, evoking Wittgenstein's illustratively nonsensical question of "whether the good is more or less identical than the beautiful."[2] But we are not dealing with logic here, and the apparent absurdity of an identicalness that is gradable into "more" or "less" does make sense in relation to Lee's poems. It will be useful here to turn our attention to Walter Benjamin's groundbreaking essay "The Task of the Translator," a piece that has directly influenced Lee's thought and writing. In an interview that I conducted with Lee for the Australian magazine *Rabbit*, she stated "I am indebted to Benjamin for convincing me that my poetry contains not simply that which is already apparent in it but also a latent generativity that might appear only through translation."[3] For Benjamin, the process of translation facilitates partial access to the realm of "pure language" that subtends the original text. This "pure language" is a kind of linguistic plenitude, wherein expression is not limited by the strictures of a particular language. Anyone who has spent a considerable amount of time translating and re-translating a poem from one language to another will know what Benjamin means when he says that it is "the task of the translator to release in his own language that pure language which is under the spell of another, to liberate the language imprisoned in a work in his re-creation of that work."[4] Unquestionably, there are vectors and dimensions within texts that are not obviously *present* in the original, non-translated versions.

But while Benjamin is undoubtedly right in pointing out that translation can liberate caches of constitutive material from an original text, it could be argued both that his diagnosis doesn't go far enough and that his nomenclature is in a certain regard misleading. My own sense, which I felt especially keenly while translating Lee's poems, is that there is an essential *impurity* to literary language, one that would remain even if all possible languages were able somehow to resound simultaneously and to compensate for each other's deficiencies. Paul Ricoeur can be a useful reagent to Benjamin's thinking on this point. Ricoeur writes that "Every language's struggle with the secret, the hidden, the mystery, the inexpressible is above all else the most entrenched incommunicable, initial untranslatable."[5] As for Benjamin, there is for Ricoeur something "hidden" in every language; however, what is hidden is not something that might be theoretically explicable into an ultimate purity—because of the incredibly complex, contradictory, and context-dependent ways in which any given living language functions, "no universal language can succeed in reconstructing its infinite diversity."[6] The upshot is that for understanding to take place, there must already be an "internal translation" that occurs within a specific linguistic community.[7] As the philosopher Richard Kearney elegantly puts it, we "are dealing with both an alterity residing outside the home language *and* an alterity residing within it."[8] Yet while Ricoeur so perspicaciously lays all of this bare, he still describes the "initial untranslatable" as a product of the "multiplicity of languages".[9] Can we not go further still and say, however oxymoronically, that the "initial translatable" is a product of language *as such*, something that would be immanent even in a sole, pre-Babelized, perfect language?

Here, we need only look at poetry itself. Good poetry is not ambiguous or equivocal by accident: ambiguity and equivocation are part of its very essence. This fact would surely still obtain if there were only a single, *perfect* language—unless of course poetry itself were somehow obviated by the perfection, rendered a mere vessel for the conveyance of information. While Benjamin describes the crude impulse to relay information as the "hallmark of bad translations,"[10] for Ricoeur, value judgments are more complicated:

> The faithfulness/betrayal dilemma claims to be a practical dilemma because there is no absolute criterion of what would count as a good translation. This absolute criterion would be the *same meaning*, written

somewhere, on top of and between the original text and the target text. This third text would be the bearer of the identical meaning, supposed to move from the first to the second. Hence, the paradox, concealed behind the practical dilemma between faithfulness and betrayal: a good translation can aim only at a supposed equivalence that is not founded on a demonstrable *identity* of meaning. An equivalence without identity.[11]

Throughout his writings on translation, Ricoeur regularly invokes the absence of a tertium (or, as above, "third text") as evidence for an insuperable theoretical impasse between two languages. But if we believe that the "initial untranslatable" is immanent in language *as such*, without reference to a second language even being necessary, then what happens to this tertium? Where vital poetry is concerned, I would argue that the tertium is already subsumed in the poem itself as a product of the work's inherent ambiguity and equivocation, and even if we cannot see this tertium, we can sense it. We can thus invoke Ricoeur's "equivalence without identity" to ask to what degree a poetic text is equivalent *to itself*.

Lee's collection is an exemplary text about which to ask the above question. Its title, with the absence of an object to which to tether the averred likeness, suggests that what characterizes the poetry therein is likeness *tout court*—a likeness that can thus also be reflexive. But of course, if a poem can be described as being *like* or *just like* itself, then it must also, in a certain regard, be *unlike* itself. If there is a latent generativity within a poem—if, as I have suggested, there are allopoems within it—then we must conclude that it is not simply *through translation* that comparison becomes possible; translation is simply the activity that, in making the latent apparent, best brings into relief the conditions for the comparison.

II. Requisite Apologia

However much a translator may feel compelled to explain or defend their decisions, it is seldom feasible to be exhaustive—it will not be possible here to talk about every interpolation, excision, or divergence in *Just Like*. I hope, therefore, that some broader principles might be extrapolated from the few examples that I invoke below. One thing that certainly warrants mention is my decision to translate the title "마치" as *Just Like* rather than *As If*. Although, context depending, both of these English phrases are equally sound translations of the Korean "마치," the "Als Ob" of Lee's gnomic preface may perhaps suggest (per standard glosses of the German phrase and the philosophical discourse that attaches to it) that *As If* would have been the more appropriate translation for this book. But of course, language tends to do its own thing, and the phrase "as if" has come to take on strong frequencies of sarcastic incredulity in colloquial English. And while I certainly believe that translators must be amenable to letting in new resonances during the process of translation, they should also be judicious as regards what gets admitted, and the resonance in question seems too shrilly incongruous for the context. What is defection in one particular is thus often fidelity in another.

It is also worth touching briefly upon the general tone of the translations. I have always read Lee's poems as being somewhat clinical, even though they never assume the kind of rigid precision that this condition might imply. Certainly, unlike most lyric poetry, Lee's poems are not subservient to an overriding anthropocentric impulse. All the same, they retain an organic suppleness that should not be jettisoned. The tone I favored for these translations is therefore slightly cold and detached while still, I hope, malleable enough to capture the proliferative energies of Lee's poetry. In terms of how the punctuation mediates this tone, it was largely a case simply of following Lee's suit: I mirrored Lee's full stops exactly, and I more or less did the same with her commas, adding my own only when the absence of a comma would introduce a strongly equivocal note not present in the source poem. Certain lexical or syntactic features of my translations (e.g. a preponderance of non-contracted words or the deployment of slightly formal-sounding absolute constructions) were also put in the service of this tone. It is perhaps worth noting that I had the privilege of alighting on this tone in isolation. A natural impulse when beginning to translate a poet is to contrast one's translations with existing ones, but I could find no English translations of Lee's poems when I embarked on this project. [12] Though an absence of antecedent translations can in a certain respect be daunting, it also removes the risk of the poet's voice being already cauterized by an "authoritative" precedent.

Especially important to mention are the twinned categories of error and defection, both of which should be borne in mind when approaching this (or any) poetic translation. It is almost certain that some mistakes will have crept into *Just Like*. To the captious critical eye, mistakes are often one of the main criteria by which a translation might be judged to be "deficient" or "bad." The truth, though, is that mistakes can be found in the work of even the best and most vital translators—a critic who is inclined to find errors will certainly be able to do so. Just as the translator should be willing to forgo the hubris of imagining that they will at all times have a full purchase on accuracy, so the critic should be cognizant of the fact that being wrong is not always "wrong." Don Mee Choi, one of the most important translator-thinkers of our time, has written the following about wrongness:

> I think I was wrong, to begin with, because I was Korean, but when I first came to the States, people constantly tried to correct my English spelling and pronunciation. My British English was wrong because it was uttered from a mouth attached to an unexpected face, a wrong face. So naturally I have become intrigued with displaced things— things that are wrong. And translation is in a perpetual state of being wrong because it isn't the original.[13]

Choi reminds us not only that wrongness is inevitable, but that sometimes we must get things "wrong" on purpose.[14] Whether unwitting or deliberate, wrongness is frequently a corollary of the distance between the source language and the target language—or rather, of the translator's attempts to traverse this distance. For centuries, a key point of contention (usefully codified by Friedrich Schleiermacher, even though it certainly preceded him) has been whether translations should be *alienating* or *naturalizing*—that is, whether they should incline more towards the source language or to the target language:

> Either the translator leaves the writer alone as much as possible and moves the reader toward the writer, or he leaves the reader alone as much as possible and moves the writer toward the reader.[15]

It isn't simply a case of one of these approaches being more faithful than the other; as per some later nomenclature proffered by Eugene Nida, equivalence can be either *formal* or *dynamic*.[16] A formal equivalence may well instantiate a broad overlap (formally and semantically) with the source text but at the cost of sounding jarring in the target language. A dynamic equivalence may well (through looser, more localized language) come closer to eliciting a reader response that is similar to the reception-context of the source text, though it may also in the process sacrifice some of the formal and semantic intricacies at play. Neither of these choices will necessarily be ethically neutral: a translation that is excessively naturalizing risks a descent into parochialism, whereas a translation that is excessively alienating risks an unseemly exoticization of the source language.

The problems consequent to the above binarisms have inevitably meant that there have emerged translation or translation-adjacent praxes that value deviation as much as or more than equivalence. There are vernacular "transcreations" of Sanskrit classics; "feminist interventionist translations" that upend baked-in patriarchal assumptions; "translucinations" that intergraft the foreign and the domestic; "faithless translations" that take linguistic incommensurability as one of their constitutive conditions; and even "fake translations" that are not linked to any extant text by the writer to whom they are ascribed. [17] If the given contextual framing is right, there is no reason why any of these strategies of defection shouldn't be considered legitimate. At the same time, the attempt to facilitate a faithful encounter with a poet should not be considered passé; the aim of conveying a poet into a new language (with sufficient fidelity that a reader who does not know the source language might still be capable in some measure of *reading* this poet) is a worthwhile one. Ultimately, the task that I set myself with this translation was to create a text that would be uncompromisingly *like* Lee's book without ever purporting to be *the same* as it.

To the above end, one thing that I found useful to think about was the different ways in which Korean and English function. Korean is a far more morphologically rich language than English, and it is capable of economically encoding a wide array of nuances relating to register or mood. Such differences can sometimes be so extreme as to thwart notions of adequation *a priori*. An obvious example is the speech level system of Korean, whose honorifics and addressee-lowering forms do not travel at all felicitously into English. To my mind, the same can also be true of some of the language's realis moods, its subtle interrogatives, and its miratives (verbal inflections that express surprise). Regarding these particulars, some considerable tonal loss is inevitable during translation. On the other hand, there are some aspects of Korean (such as the elided subject) that I think can carry over well from challenging Korean poetry into challenging English poetry, even if the elisions are not necessarily unnatural in Korean. From the opposite end, there are things that English has at its disposal that Korean doesn't have: in particular, a comparative richness of articles and number declensions. For me, it was not simply a question of downplaying the Korean features while accentuating the English ones (or vice versa); I paid no particular fealty to an alienating or naturalizing impulse. Instead, I simply leaned into whichever particularities of either Korean or English I felt worked well for the poems, sometimes allowing features of the Korean to pass like phrasal or grammatical calques into the English, at other times allowing English-language particularities to suggest new reverberations or inflections in the original.

My approach has at times created a certain degree of noise that is not there (or is *differently* there) in the original poems. Consider the below excerpt from "four-lane road":

> The four-lane road spreads like a contagion. Spreads in front of the eyes. Glistening all the while in the sun. On the four-lane road are people wearing shorts between the legs of people putting up billboards and people frozen with billboards tar slides down. The four-lane road extends out and seems to have go firsted and seems to have don't goed [. . .]

In the fourth sentence, I strove to approximate the freneticism and breathlessness of the Korean original. However, doing so required that the image be torqued somewhat. In the original, the main ganglion of ambiguity occurs around the detail of "people putting up billboards and people frozen with billboards," wherein Lee brilliantly foreshadows the denoted freezing-together via the suggestion of a compound noun ("people billboards"). This feat is achieved via a highly disruptive comma elision between "people" and "billboards," and if we imaginatively reinsert a comma at this juncture we can cleave the compound noun and make the syntagm more readable. Because it is not possible to render such a compound into English while still leaving room for the line to be resolvable into sense, I instead opted to omit a conjunction ("people wearing shorts [and]"). The result, I hope, is a sentence that can parse grammatically while still allowing for a pictorial equivocation comparable to that of the original (even if the particular chains of ambiguity are different). Another instance of noise from the same excerpt can be seen in the "go firsted" and "don't goed" formations, which are perhaps more protrusive than their Korean counterparts. In Lee's poem, the sonic patterning allows the implication of reported speech to be resolved quite easily, despite the atypical grammar. Even so, there is technically no ascription of *saying* in Lee's words; rather, there is a subsumption of uttered language into the form of a verb. Some might argue that such notes are too subtle in Korean to warrant amplification in English and that the better approach would be to mute or downplay them for a smoother translation. But because I wanted to retain the implication of an utterance denuded of actual speech—a nuance that felt appropriate, given the implied non-human agent of the utterance—the aural protrusion seemed to me an allopoetic resonance worth indulging.

Though such choices may be tendentious, this very tendentiousness raises an important question concerning the allopoetic: namely, if the specific configurations of a given language seem not to invite particular translation choices, does that necessarily mean that such choices are precluded? Is it legitimate to convey a subject elision into English when, in the Korean, the subject is either implied or is ambiguous in a way that is more endemic to the poetic conventions of the source language than to those of the target language? Is it okay for an English translator to take a highly protean approach to articles and grammatical numbers, even though the Korean poem is not—and indeed, *cannot be*—comparatively protean as regards these particulars? Questions like these return us to Benjamin's thinking about the imprisoning dimensions of individual languages. Given that certain English solecisms such as "seems to have don't goed" cannot be reliably encoded in Korean as probable translations, we might conclude that the Korean source poems are necessarily closed off to such solecisms. But such is far from the case if the mode is a consciously allopoetic one. Sometimes, the allopoetic choice might be justified via a mere cognitive inversion. For instance, we might ask how the English "seems to have don't goed" would be translated into Korean. At other times, the license may come not from any local equivalence in the source language but rather from the broader ambiance or grain of the poetry (in "person doing gymnastics," for instance, the article and number shifts were governed by the general nominative slipperiness of the poem). If some of my choices may seem in isolation to foreclose certain potentials, I hope that the opposite might be true when these choices are considered in their aggregation.

Taken on their own terms, Lee's original poems and my translations of them will certainly exhibit local discrepancies. Some parts of my translations will congeal where there is not a corresponding congelation in the Korean, just as other parts of them will flow where the Korean is more static. But what I think Lee's book shows us is that her poems—or at least her *given* poems—should not simply be taken on their own terms. As the critic Bo-Won Kang has insightfully written:

[D]espite all its difficulties, translation will not ruin Lee's poetry, because the words and sentences in her poems are optimized in the first place not for preservation or conveyance but destruction. They attempt to lose direction, and translation will help them do so. . . . One day we will read Lee Sumyeong's poems translated back into Korean from their translated versions, without reference to the originals. [18]

I read Kang's lines with a pleasurable recognition. I am content for there to be some loss or even some "destruction" in my translation of Lee's poems since loss is an ineluctable condition of the poems themselves. If such is to a degree true of all poems, it is *especially* true of Lee's poems. This very "optimization" was one of the things that emboldened me to undertake a serious translation of Lee's poetry in the first place. While the spurious notion of a *definitive* translation had already long been anathema to me, such distaste was not enough in itself. Before I could immerse myself diligently in the act of translation, my resistance to the definitive needed to be complemented by a feel for the allopoetic. I needed first to be shown the allopoem. I needed to be shown poetry that was *just like* itself—and thus, by extension, *unlike* itself. Such is what Lee's book showed me. My hope for this translation is that it might be capable, in its way, of showing something similar.

I.

THINGS LIKE CEMENT VEGETABLE PAPER

A man runs a field and the field of the man running the field caves in. A man lacking a caved-in field to the man runs. Things like cement vegetable paper sweltering he haphazardly plucks cabbage. Picks up the cabbage and walks the field a man bored through.

The mice escaping the field to escape the field is uncomfortable.

A man runs a field and because the field has no lid the era of the field closes the man. Closes the field. The man running the field drags over the field. The field is an expanding use. Into the man the man is ousted. Brings up things like cement vegetable paper.

FOLLOWING YARN

This yarn is soft. This snowfall is warm. Someone threw this yarn and now no one can use it. What to do with this yarn the fish not stopping the fish flitting around. Dragging and being dragged this yarn flits. Goes forwards and backwards. On this shelf has been put absolutely nothing. This snowfall fulfills wishes. Inside snowfall is nothing. Inside yarn has entered absolutely nothing. Yarn goes forwards and backwards. Fashions no shape. This yarn cannot be picked up. This sunshine unravels. This yarn unravels. Just endlessly unravels. This yarn does not reconcile. Not going inside it moves around donning a ball of yarn.

FOUR-LANE ROAD

The four-lane road spreads like a contagion. Spreads in front of
the eyes. Glistening all the while in the sun. On the four-lane road are
people wearing shorts between the legs of people putting up billboards
and people frozen with billboards tar slides down. The four-lane road
extends out and seems to have go firsted and seems to have don't goed

when the four-lane road spreads fully out stop up the road and
stand there

on the four-lane road drive cars that drove the roof and sometimes
the roof collapses to pick up the roof went in and throw away the roof
the four-lane road is fallen into some crucible. Tries to go eastwest like
crazy. Strives to remain at eastwest. Congealed with excitement. The
four-lane road smells strongly of petrol. Must in this way completely
evaporate

tries to put down
the loaded goods the entire transit of the ground

WHAT'S THE REASON

What's the reason, was about to enter crumpled shoes when because causes remain safe, the corpses are constantly rustling days. The bone dislocates omnidirectionally spreading the arm further out. Budding is a lonely thing. I couldn't manage to spit any then swallowed all at once. Today I really didn't want to swallow a thing. Today the remains of the vanquished, because reasons are gathered without caution, whenever asking my thoughts my thoughts will become possible. Possibility will gather and groan. The same breath that at last covers up the face

SOMEONE BRIEFLY

Woke slowly. Woke crying. Tears fell without reason from within sleep. The shoulders are scattered. Who was crying who was briefly hidden there are times even when I'm a girl times even when morning becomes perforated. When morning appears give me morning. Well-known costumes were invariably established I keep wanting to be your costume. Since the future initially passed we continued to use the future. Throwing the beach ball the girls are reiterated and who was briefly hidden who was crying I want to be your empty beach ball. Today misplaced sleep. I fit wherever.

MOST OF HIM

Most of him is without shadow. It would be good to set him down for now. Good to drape a line of him on the road.

Most of him crowds into other people. Enters and bends. Most of him unthinkingly cuts his throat. He is absently drained.

Raising a hand unawares most of him has forgotten himself. Is forgetting and raising a hand. He will get better now. The hand will stiffen. Will commit crimes.

He is discovered all at once. To mark the location
he is completely indifferent. Beats against the roof of the mouth. Giggles intertwine.

Most of him moving he does not claim movement. He moving the movement has gone cold. Perhaps he is buried in the ground. Most of him being no more than most of him mostly from the broken center

he stands trying to forget what is forgotten.

PERSON DOING GYMNASTICS

I have the gymnastics. Have the gymnastics that memorize me. I and gymnastics must arrive together.

Digging the ground the gymnastics is standing. Cutting through the dry grass and laughing along with other grasses. Dialect pours out all at once. The gymnastics are standing between the atmospheric floor and the floor.

Will I keep following the gymnastics
in becoming something slippery

I do not leave gymnastics
and I blurt out a command.

The gymnastics are bored. When gymnastics bends into me I beat gymnastics.
Gymnastics beat me.

The floors below and above drop off at the same time. I'm so noisy. I had to hide the gymnastics or they had to hide me.

Like that all at once there are fossilized optics. There, the person doing gymnastics does not appear.

The gymnastics is pointing out the atmosphere that I lack.

Gymnastics stand what with having collapsed.

WE THINK QUIETLY

A broken branch is good

broken branches crawling around are good
crawling around then being unable to become branch again is good
while reducing today's orientation

we set the dinner table where orientation pools.
On the dinner table fingers laid out all at once and eyelashes
sprouting all at once
cannot go far and
fingers being crushed in their seats of their own accord are good

will use nicknames and create friction.
Are you putting your hands there
into the place where your meal is disappearing
the now subsiding siren long since subsided.

We think quietly.
Into the place where thought is disappearing
we thread sizeable greetings into a string
for things being left in the form of
Mondays and Fridays.

For cooling things being left in some form

branches appearing from somewhere and crawling around
indiscriminately on the dinner table are good
    small cheeks that quickly tire and sweat are good
    before even becoming cheeks
    our grimacing belief is good

    on top of belief we first lie down.

CLIMBED A TREE

Climbed a tree climbed alone and in secret and as soon as I climbed the tree started growing crooked.

How do you make a cliff?
A cliff is made in one go and can be arrived at in one go I will call you "cliff"

ah so you maintain the tree and you are massaging the sky, wanted to know the means of fixing the sky.

The means say of closing the eyes and returning to bone

I keep reaching out. From atop the tree imagine the tree. Once again it is the having chosen a seemingly quiet place the having sighed and attempted to spend a late evening

an evening not going, maybe
uncertain as to whether the tree had long since been washed away.

OKAY AT THE BALCONY

Okay at the balcony okay though the house shakes okay whenever it shakes and when standing on the balcony you lose architecture. In the absence of architecture at the balcony

you can sleep. There is no sign of overlapping sleep at the balcony. A body coils around sleep and swells endlessly I want to be born into the body

I wake nothing. Will the head nod will the heart ache and like stones confined to an empty field the flowers display a body.

Obscenities flow out. Okay though jumping from the balcony is the simultaneous lifting of both feet just a little more the simultaneous being born the simultaneous jumping down from here to there

how strong is the wind the wind bumped into by flying birds how smooth the wind that drops the birds how safe

okay at the balcony okay to step forward once again and somewhere people reel. I face towards the unknown and adamantly reel. After architecture has passed rapidly by

OF THIS BUILDING

Looks up at the building. Entering and leaving the building is a strange thing. Being stood or

seated in the building is a strange thing.

Wanted to cry because there were so many blanks.

Drops the back.

The building unthinkingly rises. Opens all of the fingers. The floor and floor are cheerful. The moment the building spreads fully out from here to there

—You, throw away the building
do not hoist the building in the sky but

looks up at the building. Ascending and descending the building is a strange thing. Falling outside from within is a strange thing.

Blanks begin walking.

RAISE ARM

Raise arm and grass dies
you are standing. It would be nice to raise arm and haul coal
to contain in similar containers similar things
a similar arm
confused with arms of unknowable owner
imminent danger and
danger become a new unit unfurling you.
New unit new cloth
between new gradation and gradation
pointing at similar gradation and
the sense of having reconciled with someone's arm
locking his arms
would be nice whenever the arm is done, such unkind
hair chewing

pooling coal. It would be nice to shout the coal stuffed in the mouth
there being so much coal
that the progress of the answer is suddenly underway.
Raise arm and you
decide to find yet another of your arms passing by.
Arm flowing before you harden
you try suddenly to harden so that
raising soaring arm
this endless uncertainty expands endlessly and

with uncertainty becomes one side
in protest against a thing totally unknowable and
raise arm
suddenly leaf, like tree striving to possess leaves

PERSON LYING DOWN

Person lying down opens the lawn and lies down.
The grass today a soft awning

there are also crawling grasses that completely cover the ground

at the highest place the sun is shredded.
Where must the sun be placed

when it is uncertain where it should be placed
tears fall outside.

Person lying down is away from emotion
person an aspiring emotion
person alternating with emotion
person grown longer than the body

a person whose ankles are all scattered
a lawn whose leaps have all vanished
all the closely cut grass of

a mouth covered
speaking words as round as the earth.

Bent-backed people pass by.

I CONNECTED TO

I connected to. It is Tuesday and

am connected through table and chair and sofa and
cushion on sofa.
I am overstatement. Merged through long cupboard
through shelf and mirror.

Leave a blemish and
a door opens and closes and
I gouge out the door and it is Tuesday and

through the blinds a bundle of joy suddenly withers. Seems fit to
burst while withering.

I become filled. Pour Tuesday and

pour several articles of clothing.
Going around with several goods under several items of clothing.

I chew down on grass. Spend summer with grass.
I align with grass.

Choke with Tuesday.

Rampant with Tuesday.

Hammering a buzzing mind
into the wall. The mind
seems fit to burst.

My favourite window is this high.
Without turning the body
lifting the heels

I look outside.

TUNDRA

Is it because thought tries to traverse the room because some
thought is being had
    that exactly the same wall appears

    walks the room's floor.
    The room keeps going wrong.

    Some shop having opened

    shop assistants of whom I am heedless and shop assistants who pay
me no heed lead to shop assistants and

    turning this and that corner
    —Tundra

    shop assistants gathered scatter and scattered
    gather
    and shop assistants with no line of movement and

    standing ankles could not all be accommodated and
    wherever they fell it seemed ankles would take turns being revived.

    Will not blink here

    now my turn will come.

After bringing both hands together all the turns' differences
disappear and I
will become carp with neither head nor tail.

Head and tail will not be distinguished.
In doing some turn

LIKE THAT

It was an unknown village.
Will grow
I to you
you to me
remaining always unknown.

The entrance to the village was full of villagers.
People hand out flyers.
From this hand to that

flyers drift. Drift and stick to anywhere.
It will rain.
Putting on the rain
the flyers will die.

Reading the flyers.

Not taking the flyers being taken by no one
the rain falling from anywhere

wetted

like that
by a rain leaking from anywhere

crouching again in the village.
The village was difficult to know.

THIS TRUCK

Trucks pass. Pass daily. This truck passes. As bread gets baked or bread turns stale

it would be good to follow the truck hangs down from the truck and becomes the truck

went and missed the truck

it would be good to stand suddenly on the slick road it is dazzling and
when remembering nothing and raising boring head

are going where exactly

it would be good if I give me to whoever greets like this despite not knowing him

things running into the truck

while setting the truck in order
emergent bits of non-breathing lint

are going where exactly

this truck speeds along.

Moving constantly aside
the avenue does not break.

PRECIPICE

Is a precipice.

A low precipice a high one.
Mounts the precipice and

is a downflowing ditch. Lodged in the ditch. Because things lodged
upside down cannot be fully lodged it is once again a ditch becoming
lodged.

Wipes with napkin. Crumples
the napkin.

The ditch counterditches. It ditches and is counterditch. You are
defective entrails. This person is the infarction. Open the eyes and it is
a simultaneous convergence of infarction training.

The bones buried inside the person seem white to the point of
snapping. This person has a whitely landing night

while collapsing this person
carelessly discriminated bloods

is all the while bloods ascending the precipice.

Runs a shop. Can no longer run shop. Lowering this and dropping
that the high-placed goods are all at once an infarction. From good to
good infarction trainings at the same time a frozen

precipice.

This person is blood that does not turn.

Celestial bodies were easy.
Identical days today also shake off onto the ground.

Loudly someone is shouting.

SEESAW'S GAZE

Seesaw is seen again to move. Seesaw is suddenly again in place.
Again here is reaching there.
  Try breathing above the head try losing life and walking
  hiding some nap
  trying motionlessly to toy with some nap.
  Into sleep we palely joined people quitting us
  are far away from us breathing.
  Will part from seesaw until unable to know light and sound. What
I cannot know
  approaches. That which is unable to approach does.
  When it was stood outside the outside is cut down with one stroke.
  Lost all of outside.
  Again in the process of falling down to here. Again here and there
  a parched mouth.
  Try breathing the passing breath it being a place with no need to
breathe
  our seesaw being in place
  we are suddenly in place.
  Being so slow-moving a seesaw I break on good terms.
  All around skin will arrive.
  All around skin will grow adamant.
  Try to breathe try to lose breath leaning in both directions
simultaneously
  lost all differentiation. Again seesaw
  gazeless.

2.

SEVERAL TIMES

Several times I woke from sleep. Several times geographic study was shredded. At your place the hands did not roast. Several times a quarrel was placed on the stairs. It was not possible to look after each quarrel. Cheers erupted and we shared a t-shirt. The t-shirt remained afloat high up. Where is the outside conveyed back and forth from as the t-shirt billows. The outside is set down throughout the day and so if we are set down we want to open our eyes outside alone. Like a greeting that had arrived by itself I participated fairly in the alone. The alone was gathered here and there. Several times more in this way I resembled something correct.

PLAYING FIELD

I was standing in a playing field. You are recommending exercise. See the playing field expanding with exercise. People doing warm-up exercises turn their arms and turn their necks. Swallowing air is done in sequence, so exercises form a big line. I want to rotate an exercise ring an exercise ring appears and along the exercise ring my bones are totally empty. Cannot lift my face. In a playing field where exercise cannot be chased down it is fine if I keep taking off the same footsteps. Exercise returns after having tripped over a footstep. Finally I am in alignment with exercise. When I have an exercise does an inundated person rise. Does a person rise inundated. I was standing in a playing field. I seem to pass by having become an exercise I do not know.

DECIMAL PEOPLE

Count forwards
count backwards.

Where to stamp the decimal point
the decimal point is not revealed to people.

Shake the whereabouts.

Decimal people
lift ankles and

may have provided treatment to ballet.

The points that were held in the hands
may have quickly intersected.

STALL

Stall
a small stall
the stall exacerbates me.

Before I commit a stall the stall exacerbates me.
It is right that the stall be a stall possessing no space.

A stall displaying darkness
—Darkness, come here

the storm has no group so the storm is stood so the nightscape is
inviolately safe.

The storm merely sweeps the storm away.

I safely escape
the completely empty storm.

I slow safely.
Lower the body lower it further and under a metal bar

I point to the stall that I keep tumbling.

Whoever sends me back is right. The interval of a stall that I cannot know is right. The imbalance of the stall that arrives before arriving at the stall is right.

Above the head are electronic display boards
all at once finding the signal.

SLOWLY

I am currently stood slowly.
So as to understand the horizontal, slowly
today's thrown-on posture is slowly becoming polluted and so
the canna arrangement is keen.
I a person alone with folded arms
if fitting me well
if calling out among dampening weapons
today I become the weapons' prescription.
No longer going far to join somewhere.

I am stood in the opposite direction.
In the opposite direction there is scant alone.
For a long time observe slowly rippling waves.
When there is rippling the water does not occur.
Every moment walking alone reaching non-occurring space.
On this ground I am perhaps thoroughgoingly thickened.

Slowly behavior disappears.
Sometimes I see non-moving clouds.
Look at the trickling-down bricks.
It is something stopping.
I stop and my verticality is standing.
While splitting the horizontal one by one, slowly
I am walking slowly.
As if now carrying human landing

RIGHT TO THE TOP

On water being carried away
a carried-away
woodblock

an infected
woodblock

being carried away on water is called "woodblock." Persisting as
cold volume is called "woodblock." Passing through all passageways,
searching for an opportunity to drag and scatter themselves

one two ten woodblocks
the woodblocks do not awake.

Woodblocks try to possess plant skin. Do a lap of the town trying to
resemble plants. Try copying shiny mineral skin in water. Try regulating
the world's minerals. Along the outdoors

along the surface

not waking. At the surface
the woodblocks drown.
Drown into surface.

Clasping a woodblock

the clinging things rising things
things all undone

are becoming in common.
Are becoming undifferentiated from surface.

Let's hover into undifferentiated shapes
let's be here and be there

if the head-hair clings to the whole of the body let's go right to the
top

sparkle

CARRIES ME

Carries me. Momentarily carries me here. Show me the here. Even if I enter here here does not come to me. If here were to come to me I would surely touch shoulders with here at last the shoulders would surely vanish would surely connect to here here being at there there being at over there. Here is at here and there. Peels off having stuck to here and there. Vainly I tussle with morning and tussle with evening. Carries me. Carries me here. I, show me the here just once. Finally I end up overtaking here. But once again here is ahead of me. Something that has never once come here

GROUND

Birds flit past along the ground.

I was playing a jumping-down game
bumping into nothing and so the window didn't shake and I didn't
regain consciousness and so I went around humming and was nothing
but the unknown tongue of someone unknown falling
slowly

I unfold a ground.

I want to reach this
unexpected

ground before impact.

Must grow hair long enough to cover the ground take off all the
joy take off the overcoat say today I have fingers. Say I knock with the
fingers. Say fingers are sprouting

the ground issues a command and
looks at the people mercilessly perforating the ground. Pickaxe,
drill, bulldozer inevitably end up breaking the ground, being everywhere
the tools I will lend the tools.

Evenly unfolding the breath and unfolding a never-before-seen
catalog

I take orders and
wander around.

Whose back
bending it

was looking into the ground.

INTO SIGN OF ANYONE

Want to enter sign of anyone call to sign of anyone.

Set down sign of anyone. What rule is this as non-collapsing sob

as lost property

my morning most things give off gloom-body.
I am an increasing balance. Where is balance sleeplessness

people pass holding out sign of anyone.
Sign of anyone bumps into and
in missing pierces space.

Peek at opportunity and
someone's jumping down
follow the jumping-down knees takes out the knees. Sign of anyone
is missed

give me person

divided rudeness

look around like this in the looking around no sign of anyone I
raucously makes sign of anyone.

JUST LIKE

My mind is covered with dead leaves and it is
just like
the dead leaves are standing.
Just like
it seems like I'm dreaming I'm washing plates first seen in a dream
and no matter how neatly I stack the plates
just like
dead leaves will surely cover the ground
dead leaves will surely cover the ground completely
in which case in real time
in which case on the road
just like
particolored shawls from who knows where line up and
shawl-draped shoulders
just like
I'm crossing to a different day
I'm exhaling different breath and going around
just like
as if overflowing
as if endlessly inflating
in which case just like after I dream
let's go see white lambs
let's go see flocks of lambs suddenly walk out
just like
just bury the here

the here being swept away
my mind overturns dead leaves and

dead leaves will surely cover the ground
dead leaves will surely cover the ground completely
just like
as when after dreaming

NIGHT'S FORMATION FLIERS

Help night.
Through the night
unable to hear any words
the gushing night
the flowing night
the lung-piercing night
back from running errands
dropped the errands.
At the entrance to the shopping arcade were scattered outsiders.

There was a man goading a woman a woman goading a man. Say it
say it say it face screwed up say it

I will end this relationship

help night.
Constrained and wandering night
pallid night
unapproachable night
corpses on corpses
keeping tempo
chests torn.

Lettuce, crowndaisy, perilla, minari, placed in a basket. Blue things the things bluely held in place were collapsed. Lifted up and put down a basket.

> A pliant night a pliant corner
> the gleams staggering past
> from buildings not being built half-built
>
> buildings a resonant say it say it say it
>
> a say it in vain
> irrevocable night
>
> the night drives everything into the night.
> The night returns to the night and
> along with the night the night is completely full.

Red strings were going around rooting through night. The bundles that were tied to the strings the black vinyl bags were going around. The ends cut and loosened the hands were going around. Cannot lie down on night and

> no one can lie down on night.
> Help night that does not carry a form
> a formlessly
>
> opening night.

To extended hands
ungraspable night
not coming and
halted night

somewhere some too-small lizards appear. And during the night

clear the night.

COVERED A BOX

I covered a cardboard box and fell asleep.
Sleep harms and beneath sleep I will be harmed
while I become like sleep

the box having crumpled the crumpling was good and
even the crumpling after having become the box in the box was
good and
my walking habit
requested the habit and thought that the habit would end beneath
the box and
on the box nothing was written.

Covered a box and now everything will be better. Will break beneath
the box.
My ankles whose origins
were unknown would no longer bend.

Overhead will pass an elderly person with a box-stuffed wheelbarrow
countless boxes falling behind the elderly person

indefinitely

if I covered the box the box was covering me.
If I fell asleep sleep disappeared and
I disappeared before sleep and
the box was covering the disappeared person.

SHAPE OF BOY

A boy is dragged along the floor.

People passing by are good.
It is good that the people passing by
above the wall
without any news happen to change frequently.

Notices stick one after another.
Vertebrates appear one after another.
We wear our team colors and burst out laughing until
some death-defying boy becomes our predominance.
When wearing the team colors

a boy is dragged along the floor.

Recognition will be possible again.
The things we failed to recognize
will be possible somehow to recognize again.

Come let's unfold a boy
let's push a boy through

certain to have a boy's round head when falling from the roof.
Houses jutting prominently at different angles

on some floor of the houses a boy is drowned.
It will be easy to repair the boy. But a boy is dragged along the floor.

CONGESTED AREA

There are times when someone asks have you lived in this area long? If someone asks an answer is required.

I left I got away from the area

which area do flowing people flow back to

there is a different area at a different place. I hope I don't enter the place that I want there are people putting up signs in each area so I bump into area. There is an area reading under repair.

Chasing unknown

lengthy constructions

walking stooped. Must return from here I am saying but there is no voice. The road is congested and the roads are numbered. It seems I have seen the numbers a number of times.

Covered with numbers. This area these buildings these goods from the shopping complex have all put on numbers and adjoined. There are people putting numbers on backs and running. There are people looking at it and spearing forks. Forks are congested. Today at this area I finally congest.

But how exactly it had been possible to go in

OUR PROPORTION

Lay down a floor and wipe a floor.
Extend the floor.

—Unfold, Round Floor
—unfold, Round Breath
we are only enjoyment following a floor
on the side of the floor

lying like floor. Spreading arms
impartial like floor

we don't know how to tire and
are we creaking
are we creaking running a floor

—show yourself, Puddle
—show yourself, Longstanding Lung
for above a handspan and a handspan
we will lay for you a just floor

—appear, Unknowable Feathers
fallen from some tail

we are only enjoyment following proportion
standing here holding out a little of us
"we have arrived."

Raising our chins a little higher

we are perhaps speaking without touching our mouths.

DURING WHICH

I was standing all day today
widthwise
lengthwise
spread arms and

gained notoriety

shall I wear a raincoat
shall I cut into a tomato

I greet passersby
because the greetings are identically sized shapes
I think numbers will help

spread arms and exist as a snake
that passed without hesitation and then into dense scrub
vanish

height reaches nowhere

shall I fill a tube with air
become an unoccupied climate

no one is here, I alone
become width
become height

SOCIAL TIME

We are social life. Fountain does a dance in the garden. Pulling each other's arms we guide to fountain. Clasp fountain and drink fountain. Which is to say we enliven jackstones.

All focus is on a single gathering, a single scene. Disinfectant is placed here and there. Picks up tweezers and revives rumor. Does an activity beyond rumor.

We sit in a circle. Wear today's diverse clothes and

what comes with some material is good and
cuts the material and
material is blocked and

we do cooperation unknown to us. The material is non-toxic.
Non-toxic gang
hang non-toxic fingers and fingers
at once slacken and

our city plans where eagles fly around above non-toxic grass are lonely. Our public interest work is lonely.

We enroll living community. We contain no particular ingredients. We simply push ahead with the ingredients. We go to society and get better. Society has much time. Time descends to us.

Time will be a cover for us.

ALL THE WORLD'S LEAVE

Will apologize suddenly one day
let's go outside and begin our leave
when that time comes the air the following day and the day after
will not move
and not moving, the people on the floor drawing parking lines
okay, let's not draw any lines on the floor

rain will beat relentlessly on the window one day and
I will be by myself, hurrying and surprised
and when at last the road grows noisy
I will be by myself, stricken.

Without changing expression
in two minds
will bake transparent snacks
will completely forget
a lake
in which ducks appear

will as in the past be in and out of several neighbors
making and attaching huge doorbells in front of their houses.

Days of a ground that cannot be protected

continuing like now to walk into the days.

As though unfolding a flag
spreading out all the world's leave

TODAY I AM THE MOST

I peered briefly into the water and fell into the water

thought of fingertips that had caressed the juice of plants I sank
into the water

pushed out old hands from the water pushed aquatic plants

want at last to be floating upright above the water
today I am the most upright   .

lie on the water

breathe out
want to throw the pond

today I am the most
do not stand up

ENJOYABLE HEIGHT

This is how you get to the rooftop.

This is how the roof is laid widely and
the roof glorifies anything and
whatever roof it may be

flies and

the roof flies away.

Reasonless heights
are doing the high jump.

3.

WEATHER FORECASTER

Today strong winds will be accompanied by rain nationwide. Steam comes out of this kettle. Covers the steam with the palm of the hand. White butterflies pass by drawing striped patterns. Water flying water scattering a shore disappears. Some knifetrail has no direction. Nasty steam is a white stance. There is a stance that cannot be stroked. Yet it is stroked. Even long from now it will remain unknown what the breath let out into the air is. Birds have no feathers and people are suspending arms imperfectly.

TODAY AH THAT REMINDS ME

Today ah that reminds me I have a promise to keep. Put on new gloves and feel my forehead. The promise is ashamed. Cannot lie down next to the promise. Like this I want to stay with the plants that pump out plants. Want to scrub the plants until dyeing the hands blue. Any stuck-out tongue is blue when the promise is activated.

Today ah that reminds me I have no character. Do not have today's manners. I unthinkingly want the cruise ship's floating manners. Want to confess the cruise ship's being swept away faster than the water. But the water has already exploded so I cannot go inside if today could just be manners so I could go inside

PEOPLE STACKING BRICKS

There are people stacking bricks.

If you are picking up bricks then bricks are smooth and bricks are polite.

You can stick the bricks together
but how do you stick the bricks

there are bricklayers standing on the bricks are people who cannot move before the bricks do.

When a building stops
the building tries to say something but
it says nothing.

How many blocks must you pass by
there are things that have frozen. There are things that have been switched are things that have stuck to each other. There are things that cling fast are butterflies that have crouched down.

There are strange signs stuck to the building strange signs that cannot be learned.

RESIDENTS

Angry at residence
residents are gathered. Complex 1 complex 2

into a complex into a complex
crying children enter and because the complex spills out

there are so many complexes so
they are living in the same complex
Beautville Pineville Lornville
tying the villes and tying the hair and had a headache.

Strange-looking ballpoint pens have fallen. They are far away from
a classroom that with sufficient encouragement had developed good
handwriting and could spell its name. Ink becomes ink that does
nothing and becomes ink that sets no ballpoint pen upright and stains
no hand and is a night kicked by anyone made by anyone.

Complexes have formed long lines left and right as though trying
to repel the air. When the sun descends unexpectedly in the distance
no word is given despite the complexes not being illuminated. When
no word is given the news that no word is being given arrives and word
spreads. Men spread and women spread and men and women spread.
They have a meeting and are angry and while having a meeting they are
angry and

are crowded and they crowd and divide the classes again. Class 1 and class 2 are the same class they are house numbers 1 and 2

they are the same class but it is unclear whether they are the same house but they are the same class

the residents look like a residence.
They look like the morning paper and the evening paper.

The morning paper becomes the evening paper and the morning complex enters an older

complex and beyond the complex new complexes

surge emitting strange imposing screams. Residents keep taking out the new complex and patrolling the old complex and circling the same ville and

everything will be okay.

Finding out their accommodation will be difficult.

They lay planks and there are people lying down and because they touch some of the planks to the bodies the planks become signs and become specimens and become tickets and the timetables the number slips the name cards go around

between the complexes where complex 1 complex 2 accumulate the pipes buried in the walls accumulate and

residents rush
bodies blurred

the residents are flawless. The residence's contempt is flawless.

While keeping daily appointments with each other residents share grievances about the discomfort of residence.

Get along perfectly.

FACTORY RESULTS

In the middle of the city there are factories.
Factories extend in every direction.
What flows from the factories is a hyper-precise leveling out

will find

an air full of winged insects. Will find winged insects.

It takes no time. Factory operation truly captivates us. The running
of a factory from the air

has previously met with swarming supplies. The supplies
can't come in from where they came and
the supplies don't know which side they should stand and

when coiling around each other between factories
we had no hair.

Let's just do it like that

in the middle of the factory swiftly flying descending floating let's
become sawdust forming into heaps sawdust heaping up to our necks
until the sawdust has heaped up let's garble our words without realizing
we are dizzy

captivated by the factory as a result of the factory
not knowing how to do it

covering hands and feet

new orders will pour in.

MIDNIGHT IS COMING

Midnight is coming. Midnight passes.

All at once extracted floating buildings
count one by one the buildings.
Is a building.

Slip off the head and
coming and going
a shriek of unknowable owner scatters.

A midnighted corridor does not cross paths. In a fixed direction is
useless.
No one knows how to close the corridor.

Sets fixed intervals in corridor and hostages are standing.
The hostages throw cabbage to each other.
Hostages are thickly fattened.

The cabbage is vivaciously still and
cabbage flies around falling to pieces.

When midnight passes
when midnight is in common
midnight is clearest.
Leaves of unknowable owner green everywhere.

ALL AROUND

You are made
all around.
Made right now.

You are even made at all.

An inevitable stem

enforcing the method of growing into stem. Escaping into stem.
Throwing bush in the air.

Lying down in a livestock enclosure. It is fine to widely mark the
enclosure and enter it.
Snooping around today's new frame
which is like livestock which are like a newly built enclosure for
livestock.
A certain posture succeeds in going into livestock.

You will seal up the livestock.

An inevitable excursion

where did it submit you

you have straightened up your body

all around.
Caught the body.

You are parallel with the air's muscles. You stand back
all around.

An inevitable interior

you add just one line of nap.

ALMOST REALISTIC

I received vitality. Out on the street
the street has sprung up of its own accord and
aimlessly running kids
knock me down and

an almost rational bird
is totally empty.

My posture that was as if facing almost frontwards
is inviolately spatial.

Would spend evenings sitting on the bannister eating jam-filled
bread. Picked up evening and flew away or picked up the bannister and
flew around or

flew somewhere

come in

—White, Black Keys
Empty Keys
let's sing an almost great facileness

the keys move and
the notes are on bad terms.

Don't listen and don't answer and

how are the notes always revived

almost realistic
do the vivacities jostle for prominence and expand

GUESTBOOK

You are unopening leaves. Leaves flying leaf not being flown leaf
stuck on a window are so many windows.

On this street the thing pressing
what with your pressing the thing pressing you, you walk almost
regularly.
The head is completely empty.
Swirling in the head, a sphenoid bone
at the end of a building when footsteps chase each other down, a
sphenoid bone

found found
like a row of death-teeth is found a neatly arranged black. Black
standing and black holding nothing and
unable to hide in this dark.

The world being backless, your weeping sounds.
Backless night
backless playground

in a spineless alley
upon absently standing

until escaping this alley
what was the cry that went through this alley

alone cutting the world's epidermis

whenever you speak mud is dashed somewhere.
A person attempting mud
the appearing everywhere of mud

that which from everywhere is being delayed

LINE

Where did this line come from want to be engulfed by the line

unknowable processions

processions escaping processions overflowing stands on which
processions gathered stands
covering the stands

I run wildly.
Run from within
the line in ignorance of the line.
Being the place where the line occurs

waiting turns
people tear from bush and put in mouth
people grow in height

I fight with an omnipotent hedge. The hedge is level. The hedge is
in disarray. The hedge gets.

Exhibit
hedge exhibit
expanding

line.

Holed leaves simultaneously
moving holes

on breaking the line follow the line.

YOUR FORM

Please show your form

you are laughing form. Are the intention to laugh. Where did you
come from

laughing despite having asked
how do you throw laughter
when unease starts

unease your cheerfulness
the ceiling is high and you are jumping down from it laughing. Days
that no one knows seem to be over there. You spread the days.

From high places to low places from low places to high places
following the wall around I too will assume the form of days

—Forms, unite

running forms

will perhaps
resemble the walking of straw
resemble the crying of straw

today my form is good. It is good that my form is with me.

Please show your form, you
abundant.

INTERVIEW BETWEEN COLIN LEEMAR-SHALL AND LEE SUMYEONG

Colin Leemarshall: It might be useful to begin this interview by asking about your general orientation to poetry. I feel that many of your poems are defiantly *anti-poetic* in their eschewal of the most enduring lyrical seductions—affective content, heightened diction, portentous lineation, etc. The above framing is of course crude and expedient, but it might help to hint at a certain tenor of poetic renunciation in your work. How do you feel your poems are working *with* or *against* poetry writ large?

Lee Sumyeong: Whether my poetry is deemed poetic or anti-poetic will depend upon one's point of view. Certainly, if my work is gauged in terms of the usual lyrical seductions, it might appear anti-poetic. The major lyrical staples—appeals to the emotion, say, or language that attains to poetic refinement through metaphorical or symbolic figuration—are things that I usually avoid. For me, emotion in poetry is frequently a spurious means of trying to expand the self (or an equivalent privileged agent), and metaphorical and symbolic figuration are often mobilized simply to bolster the self's connection to the world. Such features are characteristic of traditional lyric poetry, whereas my own poetry moves closer towards an attenuation, an abandonment, or even an erasure of the self. Even where the self appears in my poetry, my aim, however futile, is to instantiate a kind of parity between self and object rather than to subjugate object to self. I believe that my work can be said to be poetic—to be working *with* poetry. However, such a claim may require a definition of poetry that can accommodate both a renunciation of the familiar lyrical seductions and a pursuit of new intimations or articulations in relation to objects.

CL: Your poems seem to foreground their surfaces—by which I mean to say that they are characterized by a certain immediacy and idiosyncrasy that marks them almost immediately as Lee Sumyeong poems. I'm thinking, for instance, of the matter-of-factness of the poems' propositional frames, the relentlessness of their explications, and the deceptive simplicity of their diction. How do you conceive of the surfaces of your poetry, and to what extent do you feel that these surfaces are in tension with the latent content of the poems?

LS: One commonly hears that poetry gives expression to things that are unseen, thus allowing us to apprehend them. Typically, the implication here is that unseen human interiorities, conceptions, or morals are revealed through allusive textual objects. According to this view, then, the truly important content is not visible; what's visible is simply the array of objects have been mobilized in the service of revealing the anthropic thought and meaning.

Personally, I'm not particularly partial to this kind of thinking. The more one emphasizes the unseen, the easier it becomes to give primacy to humans over objects—to privilege a self or a primary agent. The opposite approach allows one to better apprehend the objects or phenomena on the other side of the poem—the things that could collectively be described as constituting the poetic surface. This surface represents a direct and unmediated world as it exists before being tinged by human conceptualization; a world of objects that cannot be read or ordered according to "sense"; a world, ultimately, that can no longer be interpreted or known according to our familiar patterns. I attempt to write the world of the unknowable surface. For me, poetry is essentially an attempt to escape from the abyss of meaning and into surface.

At the same time, poetic language is not occluded or impassive—it responds to the signals generated by the expressivity of syntax. Therefore, poetry must also move beyond the surface and to the other side. However much we might attempt to escape anthropic interpretation, it is difficult to resist the centripetal force of meaning as it is generated through syntax. So while my poetry is certainly oriented towards surfaces, it might also be thought to be embroiled in a conflict with latent meanings and interpretations. You could say that my poetry is animated by a desire to elude meaning at the very moment that meaning seizes hold of it.

CL: One of the things that most strikes me about your poems is how fluid and fertile their grammar can be. They often take advantage of the rich morphological possibilities of the Korean language in order to problematize or ambiguate grammatical properties such as agency, antecedence, number, and so on. This effect is doubly striking in that the poems simultaneously evince a countervailing impulse towards clean, unimpeachable syntax. Is there anything in particular that attracts you to this vacillation between fluid and static grammars?

LS: In most writing, the image and the message are fused so as to facilitate understanding, but I tend instead to be captivated by detached images that resist understanding—that is, images that not only refuse to prop up the message but that strive to do away with the message altogether. In particular, I respond to images that grow more impervious to the message as they increase in clarity. One way of lending clarity to images is through precise syntax—exactingly constructed sentences can enable images to become more vividly animated.

The more fluid and fertile grammatical aspects of my poetry are likewise trained towards the image—but they are concerned with capturing a different dimension of the above-mentioned dichotomy. Because the message is a product of comprehension, the image must be freed from comprehension before it is emancipated from the message. Unbound from comprehension, the freed image is no longer static, so expressing it in its flux sometimes necessitates transforming syntax and defecting from established grammar. In other words, for the image to remain live, the grammar must respond to the movement of the image and open up to each moment accordingly.

I don't think that my poetry roves back and forth from precise to fluid syntaxes just for the sake of it; rather, I see the movement as an inexorable response to the live images of each moment, an attempt to delineate these images through language. I do of course enjoy the vacillation—although it's perhaps worth saying that the two grammatical poles may not actually be that far removed from each other.

CL: I notice that the vocabulary of your poetry is, etymologically speaking, preponderantly Korean. Specifically, there is a high proportion of native Korean words relative to Sinitic words (the latter of which, so I understand, comprise a higher percentage of the language's lexical stock). I feel that such determinedly "Korean" texts have an uncanny valence since they at no point seem to represent a patriotic vaunting of the vernacular. Might you care to elaborate on your seeming preference for pure Korean words in your poems?

LS: Abstract nouns in the Korean language are predominantly derived from Chinese characters. Such words might be thought of as semantic or conceptual vessels. The reason that there are comparatively few Sinitic words in my poetry is that I am not really drawn to abstract nouns. My preference is instead for poetry that privileges image above reason. Consequently, I prefer the Korean to the Sinitic, the colloquial to the literary, and the mundane to the abstract. Sinitic words, literary language, and abstraction work well as vessels for conveying fixed concepts, while their opposites are better as preventatives against the congelation of meaning.

There's also another reason. Korean words, colloquialisms, everyday terms, and the like collectively form a kind of language pool that can be drawn from in order to bypass literary schemata. I believe that literary innovation occurs when the verbal flow moves away from refined literary language (which is often full of abstract nouns) and into this "non-literary" pool. One can then renew the poetic from behind poetic language, from outside of poetry, via recourse to non-poetic influences. Although seemingly anti-poetic, such a venture can perhaps expand the scope of poetry.

CL: At first blush, the poems in *Just Like* might seem more concerned with trivial matters than with weighty political or ecological questions—and you have alluded to the importance of triviality in some of your critical writing. But I sense that such "triviality" is not impervious to the encroachments of politics and history. The "goods" in "precipice," for instance, could perhaps be read under a Marxist (or more broadly anti-capitalist) lens. I also wonder whether "things like cement vegetable paper" might be interpreted as a kind of quantum pastoral, whereby the entanglement of man and field engenders various ecopoetic resonances. Do you believe that your poems brook such readings?

LS: When writing, I certainly tend to favor triviality above big ideologies or belief systems. As things increase in triviality, I feel that they become less generalized and more variegated—and therefore less bound by limits. Naturally, there is then more room to elude interpretation or judgment. In other words, through triviality, it becomes more possible to turn away from meaning and message.

I don't think it's at all strange to read the objects in my poems under anti-capitalist, quantum mechanical, or ecopoetic lenses since my poetry doesn't overtly provide any lenses. Readers of my poetry can interpret it how they wish. If I have a hope, it's that the objects contained in my poetry are sufficiently diverse as to preclude a single interpretive lens.

CL: Have you ever wondered about the particular challenges that your poems might pose for translators? When I was translating your poems, I felt I had to take occasional liberties with the semantics in order to preserve the generative strangeness. What degree of defection do you think is permissible in a translation?

LS: "Generative strangeness" strikes me as an *a priori* condition of language, the roughness that cannot be pared down by meaning. In this respect, your term evokes Walter Benjamin's notion of "pure language." For Benjamin, pure language was not what was dissolved during translation; on the contrary, he believed it was something that came to light only *through the process of translation*. I am indebted to Benjamin for convincing me that my poetry contains not simply that which is already apparent in it but also a latent generativity that might appear only through translation.

When words are changed, the original strangeness of a text cuts through the impossibility of translation and stands in greater relief. From this point of view, the defection of translation appears unavoidable. I think that through the shock of translation, poetry can grow both more tenacious and more expansive. For me, this condition obtains equally whether the translation is "word for word" or comparatively loose.

CL: Veering slightly into biographical terrain, I'd like to ask what first drew you to writing poetry. Also, has the experience of writing poetry felt like a vocation, an avocation, or something else entirely?

LS: I can't necessarily cite this as an impetus or reason, but I have a memory of being quite young and having perhaps my first real writing experience. I was around 10 years old, and, by chance, I was home alone. Sitting down against a wall in the corridor, I found myself suddenly unable to endure the silence. So I took out my notebook and began writing—things about death and fear. I remember this experience because I was taken aback by the feeling that the situation seemed to become verbalized. I wrote "death", and it was as though I suddenly knew death intimately. It was from this point that my life writing poetry seemed to begin. A life of living through words, as it were.

Currently, I consider writing poetry to be once a job, an inclination, an experiment, and a game. Additionally, it's a strange form of perception—although it's also an enjoyment that surpasses perception. Finally, it's a record of the times when I put down everything to face myself and objects and the world.

CL: In conclusion, I would like to ask you about your relationship to Korean poetry. Do you consider yourself to be working within a recognizable lineage of experimental Korean poetry? To what extent do you consider your poetry to be in conversation with that of your Korean contemporaries? Finally, who, in your opinion, are some of the most interesting contemporary Korean poets that non-Korean readers might be completely unfamiliar with?

LS: Although its history is relatively short, modern Korean poetry has undergone dynamic transformations in a compressed fashion. Speaking crudely, one might say that things have developed with modernism and realism alternately vying for prominence. The modernist poets have tended to privilege form above content—and to opt for a more experimental style. Rather than try to invoke ideology to deal with the damaging realities of colonial history, national partition, and civil war—in addition to rapid industrialization and democracy—these poets have resorted instead to experimental aesthetics in order to approach such matters. Yi Sang, Kim Gu-yong, Cho Hyang, Kim Chong-Sam, Kim Chunsu, Kim Su Young, Lee Seung-hoon, and Oh Kyu-won each in their own ways explored questions of self, world, and language—and in the process created new poetic inflections. I consider my poetry to be both consciously and unconsciously in dialogue with that of these forebears. In my efforts to make modest inroads beyond the horizons that these writers opened up, I am led to conclude that literature and history are not separate phenomena.

When I read poetry, I try and discern current possibilities from the perspective of the past and to look for signs of obsolescence in the present. Exemplary bygone poetry can help us ascertain which modern perspectives are valid, while poetry from the contemporary era can sharpen our understanding of which sensibilities have now vanished. I try not to focus inordinately on poetry from any single era. Reading across eras might suggest paths to the poetry of the future, even if only tenuous ones.

There is currently a great diversity of poetry emerging in Korea. The poets Choi Jeongrye, Park Sangsoon, Ham Kisok, Seo Dae-kyung, Im Kyeong-seop, Baek Eun-seon, and Kim Yi Kang might collectively give a good indication of some of the variety on display. As the 21st century develops, Korean poetry continues to fissure. I think the various creative tributaries that are emerging bode well for the future.

NOTES TO THE TRANSLATOR'S INTRODUCTION

[1] Consider, for instance, the words "homoousian" and "homoiousian," which respectively refer to the conflicting Trinitarian positions of the Father and Son being of *the same* and *like* essence. Regarding this slight but crucial distinction, William Gaddis quipped in his novel *The Recognitions* that "the fate of the Christian church hung on a diphthong."

[2] Ludwig Wittgenstein, *Tractatus Logico-Philosophicus*, trans. D. F. Pears and F. B. McGuinness (London and New York: Routledge & Kegan Paul, 1961), 23.

[3] Lee Sumyeong, "Colin Leemarshall interviews Lee Sumyeong," in *Rabbit*, issue 33 (2021): 129.

[4] Walter Benjamin, "The Task of the Translator," in *Illuminations*, ed. Hannah Arendt, trans. Harry Zohn (New York: Schocken Books, 1970), 80.

[5] Paul Ricoeur, "A 'passage': translating the untranslatable," in *On Translation*, trans. Eileen Brennan (London and New York: Routledge, 2006), 33.

[6] Ricoeur, "The paradigm of translation," in *On Translation*, 24.

[7] Ibid.

[8] Richard Kearney, "Introduction: Ricoeur's philosophy of translation," in *On Translation*, xviii.

[9] Ricoeur, "A 'passage': translating the untranslatable," 30.

[10] Benjamin, "The Task of the Translator," 70.

[11] Ricoeur, "A 'passage': translating the untranslatable," 34.

[12] In the past year or two, there has been something of an efflorescence of Lee's poetry in English translation. On top of my translations, which have appeared in various print publications, translations of Lee's poems have appeared online in *Korean Literature Now* (trans. Seth Chandler), *Asymptote* (trans. Mattho Mandersloot), and *chogwa* (various translators).

[13] Don Mee Choi, "A Conversation with Don Mee Choi," in *Lantern Review Blog* (Dec. 5, 2012): https://www.lanternreview.com/blog/2012/12/05/a-conversation-with-don-mee-choi/

[14] We might locate one example of "wrongness" in Choi's "Double S Double S," a translation of Kim Hyesoon's poem "쌍시옷 쌍시옷" (ssangsiot ssangsiot) from the collection *Phantom Pain Wings* (New York: New Directions). In her translation, Choi opted to duplicate every word-initial "s" in the text ("sspace,", "sstrands", etc.). This supernumerary "s" can be considered entirely Choi's device. For while the source poem does contain a leaven of graphical suggestiveness (the digraph "ㅆ" reads almost like an ad hoc logogram for the birds in the poem), there

is no non-standard orthography in Kim's Korean. If Choi's translation is "wrong" for deploying a device that has no clear analogue in Kim's poem, though, it is simultaneously a purposive reckoning with the lacuna that opens up in the congress between the source and target languages. Any English translation of Kim's poem must not only sacrifice the avian suggestiveness of the "ᄴ" grapheme, but it must also somehow reference a sibilant that has no direct equivalent in English. If Choi had been content to deal with this problem merely via the vaguely approximate "Double S Double S," the decision would have been understandable but also somewhat attenuating. Instead, what we get is not an attenuation but an emulsion—the dispersal of the foreign throughout the English poem. If this emulsion serves as a reminder of Ricoeur's "initial untranslatable," it also brings to the fore a key allopoetic resonance—namely, the narrative and visual bleed that might occur when a particular script-sound dyad comes into contact with an incongruent linguistic system.

[15] Friedrich Schleiermacher, from "On the Different Methods of Translating," trans. Waltraud Bartscht, in *Theories of Translation: An Anthology of Essays from Dryden to Derrida*, eds. Rainer Schulte and John Biguenet (Chicago: University of Chicago Press, 1992), 42.

[16] Eugene A. Nida and Charles R. Taber, *The Theory and Practice of Translation* (Leiden: Brill, 1969).

[17] The term **transcreation** in this context was coined by the poet and translator Purushottama Lal, who himself transcreated the Sanskrit epic

the *Mahabharata* in English. A recent work billed explicitly as being in a **feminist interventionist** mode is Meena Kandasamy's partial translation of the Tamil classic the *Tirukkural*. More can be read about Kandasamy's translation in the article "Meena Kandasamy's feminist intervention on the Tirukkural," hosted on the *Himal Southasian* website:https://www.himalmag.com/meena-kandasamy-book-of-desire-feminist-intervention-on-tirukkural-tiruvalluvar/. The word **translucination** can be traced to the poetry magazine *Chain* (vol. 10: translucinación, 2003), whose Spanish subtitle was originally coined by the Chilean poet Andrés Ajens. Jena Osman and Juliana Spahr wrote in their editorial notes that translucinación/translucination is "a cross-cultural encounter loaded with hope and yet always in danger of going wrong." The poet Harry Gilonis has described his versionings of classical Chinese poetry as **faithless translations**. For some commentary on a couple of Gilonis's faithless translations, the reader is directed to "The poet as symbiont," my review of Gilonis's *Rough Breathing*, which is hosted on the *Jacket2* website: https://jacket2.org/reviews/poet-symbiont. As regards **fake translations**, some potent examples include Theresa Hak Kyung Cha's "Sappho" epigraph in *Dictée* and some of Jack Spicer's "translations" in *After Lorca*. Faker still are the "translations" of the non-existent Japanese poet Araki Yasusada, which (though never verified) are generally attributed to the notorious literary firebrand Kent Johnson.

[18] Bo-Won Kang, "The Complete Renunciation of the Exceptional," trans. Seth Chandler, in *Korean Literature Now*, vol. 57: https://kln.or.kr/magazine/magazineView.do?volumeIdx=180

ACKNOWLEDGMENTS

A number of the translations in this book have variously appeared (some of them in slightly different form) in *Rabbit, Lana Turner, Chicago Review, Firmament,* and *Mercurius.* My interview with Lee first appeared in *Rabbit,* and my translator's introduction was originally published in *Asymptote.* I extend my gratitude to Amelia Dale, Calvin Bedient, David Lau, Kirsten Ihns, Jack Chelgren, Jessica Sequeira, Marcus Silcock, Lee Yew Leong, Barbara Halla, and Sherilyn Nicolette Hellberg for working with me directly in facilitating these initial publications. For their various engagements with the poetry or the paratexts contained herein, I thank Phil Baber, Breanna Castellani, Brandan Griffin, Hee Sung Jun, and my beloved family members. Considerable thanks are due to Jake Levine for enthusiastically taking on this book, and I am indebted to him, Carrie Adams, Janaka Stucky, Charlotte Renner, and Taylor D. Waring for their skill, patience, and judiciousness during the editing of the manuscript. Special thanks to Amelia, who spurred me to initiate contact with Lee Sumyeong in the first place. My profoundest thanks to Yuna and Noelle for their love and nourishment while I was working on the manuscript. Finally, I thank Lee Sumyeong, who was a wonderfully warm and willing correspondent during the process of my translating these poems.

ABOUT THE AUTHOR

Lee Sumyeong was born in Seoul in 1965. She is the author of eight poetry collections in Korean as well as numerous critical writings and books on poetics. In addition, she has translated several texts into Korean, including books on Romanticism, Lacan, Derrida, and Joyce.

Colin Leemarshall lives in South Korea. He runs the print-on-demand press Erotoplasty Editions, which sells innovative and idiosyncratic books of poetry at cost price.

ABOUT THE SERIES

The Moon Country Korean Poetry Series publishes new English translations of contemporary Korean poetry by both mid-career and up-and-coming poets who debuted after the IMF crisis. By introducing work which comes out of our shared milieu, this series not only aims to widen the field of contemporary Korean poetry available in English translation, but also to challenge orientalist, neo-colonial, and national literature discourses. Our hope is that readers will inhabit these books as bodies of experience rather than view them as objects of knowledge, that they will allow themselves to be altered by them, and emerge from the page with eyes that seem to see "a world that belongs to another star."